THE ONE WITH ALL THE

CROSS-STITCH

21 Unofficial Patterns for Fans of Friends

ULYSSES PRESS

Published in the US by:
ULYSSES PRESS
PO Box 3440
Berkeley, CA 94703
www.ulyssespress.com

ISBN: 978-1-64604-186-2
Library of Congress Control Number: 2021931493

Printed in the United States by Versa Press

10 9 8 7 6 5 4 3 2 1

Acquisitions editor: Casie Vogel
Managing editor: Claire Chun
Editor: Renee Rutledge
Proofreader: Janet Vail
Front cover design: Flor Figueroa
Interior design and layout: what!design @ whatweb.com
Pattern maker: Anna Selezneva
Patterns: based on images provided by Shutterstock.com
Photographs: pages 10-18 © Michael Calcagno

SEPTEMBER 2021

CONTENTS

INTRODUCTION

Could cross-stitch *be* any more fun? Welcome to *The One with All the Cross-Stitch*, the first crafting book ever to include fun and friend-tastic patterns that pay homage to one of the greatest shows of all time.

The patterns in this book include some classic sayings as well as deep cuts. Only true fans (and your true friends) will know exactly why you have framed a Chick and Duck BFF cross-stitch (see page 32) or why you've stitched "Pivot" into a throw pillow (see page 28). Perfect as gifts or decor for your own "realistically" sized NYC apartment, the opportunities are endless.

If you're a beginner, be like your favorite type-A chef and make sure to thoroughly read this introduction before you hop in. There are some good tips in here to get you started. If you've stitched before, feel free to dive right in to your first pattern. Patterns are organized by difficulty.

Cross-stitch is absolutely perfect for enjoying ten seasons of laughter and love. So grab your remote and a cappuccino, and let's get stitching!

SUPPLIES

Cross-stitch is a relatively cheap craft (thank goodness!). You'll need a few essential items before you begin.

FABRIC

All the patterns in this book use Aida fabric, a loose-weave fabric perfect for stitching. At your craft store, this will come in a variety of colors and counts (most commonly 11-count, 14-count, and 16-count). The count refers to how many stitches per inch, so for a 14-count Aida fabric there are 14 stitches (or squares) per inch.

Most of the patterns in this book are designed to fit 14-count Aida fabric. A few that are a little more detailed use 16-count Aida fabric (see NYC Skyline on page 64, Lobster Love on page 72, and Grandma's Taxi on page 80).

Technically you can cross-stitch on any linen or fabric, but you'd be working without a guide. Aida is perfectly designed for all your cross-stitch needs!

You can really use whatever count Aida fabric you prefer, but it will change the final size of your project. If you use 16-count Aida fabric for a pattern that was originally designed on 14-count fabric, the pattern will be a bit smaller and the stitches will appear a lot smaller. Conversely, if you use 11-count fabric, you can make any pattern a bit bigger, but the stitches will be more visible.

EMBROIDERY HOOP

Embroidery hoops, used to help stabilize your work as you stitch, are available at your local craft store and come in a variety of sizes and materials. Each hoop has two parts: a smaller inner hoop and a larger outer hoop with a screw for tightening. Wooden and plastic hoops work just fine, although wood lends that classic look. I recommend buying a few different sizes of hoops so you have a selection on hand. If you want to display or gift your finished project in the hoop, make sure you purchase the corresponding size indicated in the pattern.

NEEDLES

The best needle for cross-stitching is called a tapestry needle. These have bigger eyes (aka the hole at the top of the needle) and a blunt tip. I recommend a size 24 tapestry needle for the 14-count patterns and a size 26 needle for the 16-count patterns.

EMBROIDERY FLOSS

All the projects in this book use 6-strand DMC embroidery floss (also known as embroidery thread). Each color has a corresponding name and DMC color code. Your local craft store should have a broad selection, but if you're having trouble finding an exact color you can substitute with one that looks similar.

Most projects only need one skein (bundle) of floss per color. I've tried to reuse colors as much as possible to avoid too much leftover floss.

Unless otherwise noted, you'll use two of the six strands whenever stitching.

> Buying floss online can be a bit tricky—it's tough to buy just one skein. There's a lot of non-DMC embroidery floss available online. Official DMC floss has the best color selection and quality, but you can use other brands. You'll have to match the colors yourself, but feel free to get creative!

EXTRA SUPPLIES

Here are a few more items to have on hand that require little explanation:

Masking tape. Aida cloth can fray easily; if you tape the edges before you get started you can prevent fraying.

Scissors. Keep your scissors handy! I love my small travel scissors. They're great for when you're stitching on the go.

Pencils. A pencil (not a pen) is good for marking the center of your fabric.

It's best practice to start at the center of any cross-stitch pattern. Before you start any project, prep your fabric by centering it tautly in your embroidery hoop. Here are step-by-step instructions for getting started with Aida fabric:

1. Starting with clean hands, cut out a piece of fabric that is at least 1 to 3 inches longer on each side than your finished pattern's length and height. I always manage to mess this up, so I err on the side of 3 inches. This gives you a little wiggle room for mistakes and framing your patterns.

2. Fold the fabric in half horizontally and crease. Fold it in half vertically and crease. The dead center of your fabric will be where the two creases meet. Mark it with your pencil.

3. Loosen the screw on your hoop until the smaller hoop is free. On a flat surface, center your fabric on top of the smaller hoop. Press down with the larger hoop to secure the fabric between the two hoops.

4. Make sure the fabric is taut and tighten the screw.

You may have to readjust your hoop depending on where you're working in the pattern. Follow these directions again, centering the part of the fabric you're working with instead of the actual center of the fabric.

This book includes counted cross-stitch patterns. That means you'll have to count how many stitches you need and then make that many, as they aren't already outlined on the fabric for you.

Each square of the pattern represents one cross-stitch. The size or shape of the box will indicate the type of stitch. A visual guide is below; see the section, Basic Stitches, for how to create these stitches.

Each square also has a color and symbol that corresponds to the pattern's key, which tells you what DMC color floss you should use. The symbols are especially helpful if you are using a black-and-white pattern or working with similar colors.

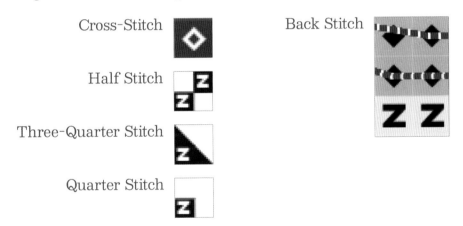

Cross-Stitch

Half Stitch

Three-Quarter Stitch

Quarter Stitch

Back Stitch

The blue grid lines indicate the dead center of the pattern. While each square has gray gridlines, you'll notice thicker lines that indicate every five stitches. There are also numbers on the top of each pattern that indicate groups of ten stitches from the center. These are all included to make counting a little easier.

KNOTTING YOUR THREAD

You can always just make a knot at the end of your thread, but I don't recommend it. It creates a messy backside and will make your project lumpy if you ever want to frame it. Here are a few alternate ways to start and end your thread.

BURIED THREAD

This is my favorite and the easiest way to secure your floss (in my opinion). This technique has no knots and gets you started ASAP.

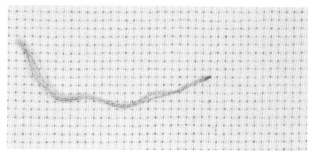

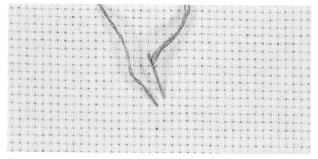

I. Cut your floss to the desired length, then thread the strands through the eye of your needle. Bring your needle and thread up through the fabric from the back, but don't pull all the way through. Leave 1 to 2 inches of tail of thread on the backside of the fabric.

2. On the front side of the fabric, insert your needle in the diagonal hole (like you are making the first leg of a cross-stitch). Pull, but do not pull your 1- to 2-inch tail all the way through.

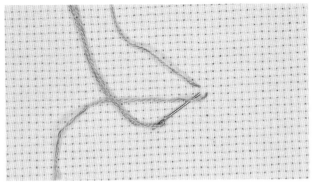

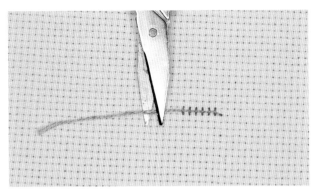

3. When you make your next stitch, make sure you capture your tail so that the loose end is secured by your next stitch. Pull the thread taut.

4.Continue stitching, capturing your tail and securing it further until it feels like it cannot come undone (usually four to six stitches). Snip off any excess tail.

WASTE KNOT

A variation of the buried thread technique, but includes a knot to make things just a bit easier!

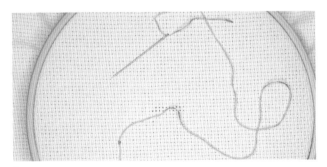

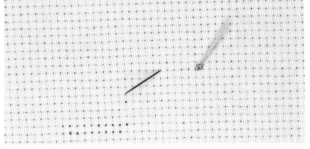

1. Cut your floss to the desired length, then thread the strands through the eye of your needle. Make a knot that cannot be pulled through your fabric. You may need to double or triple knot.

2. Starting on the front side of your fabric, insert your needle and pull until the knot catches. Pull your thread up four to six squares away.

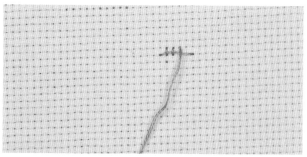

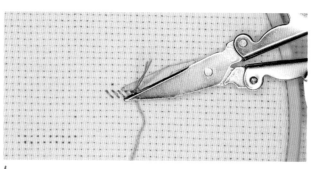

3. Start stitching toward the knot, making sure to "bury," or secure, your thread on the backside of the fabric as you work.

4. Once you reach the knot on the front side of the fabric, snip it off using scissors from the front side. Keep on stitching!

LOOP START

This is a more intermediate technique but perfect for stitchers who love a really clean backside. It only works with an even number of threads.

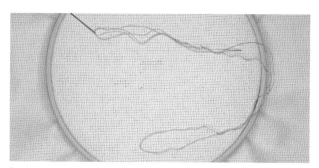

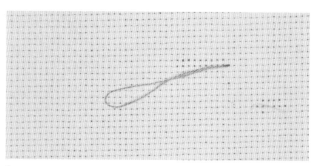

1. Using only one strand of floss, cut it to double the desired length. Bring the ends together to essentially fold it in half. Thread both ends through the eye of your needle, pull about 2 to 3 inches, and then stop. There should be a loop at the tail of your threaded needle.

2. Bring your needle and thread up through the fabric from the back, but don't pull all the way through. Leave 1 to 2 inches of thread. (Your loop should be on the backside.)

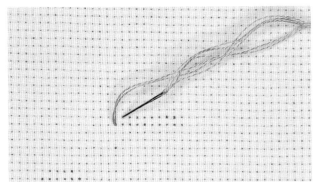

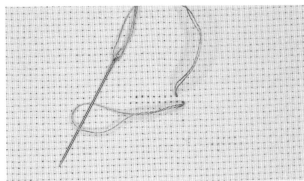

3. Make the first leg of your stitch, usually inserting into the diagonal hole for a traditional cross-stitch but do not pull taut.

4. On the backside, thread your needle through the loop on the back. Pull taut. Make sure the loop is flat before you continue stitching.

ENDING A THREAD

If you run out of thread or no longer need the color you're working with, follow the below instructions to end a thread.

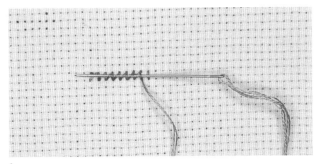

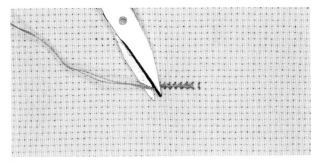

1. Flip to the backside of your fabric. Slide your threaded needle under the existing stitches; about four to six stitches will do the trick.

2. Snip off the extra thread.

BASIC STITCHES

The patterns in this book use a few different stitches beyond the traditional cross-stitch. Each stitch is outlined below. If you're ever confused about how to do a stitch, YouTube has a ton of great tutorials!

CROSS-STITCH

You'll be stitching this classic X stitch for the majority of the projects in this book.

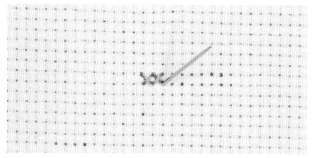 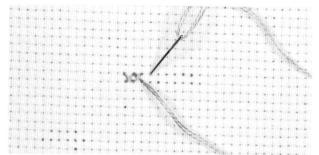

1. Draw your threaded needle up through the back of the fabric. I like to start in the bottom left-hand corner of the stitch I'm about to make.

2. Insert your needle into the hole diagonally from where you came up. Starting from the bottom left-hand corner, this would be the upper right-hand corner of the stitch, as shown in this image.

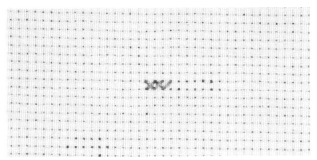

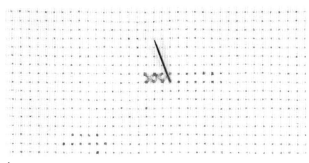

3. This is your first leg of the stitch, also known as a half stitch.

4. Draw your needle up from the back, inserting through the bottom right-hand corner hole.

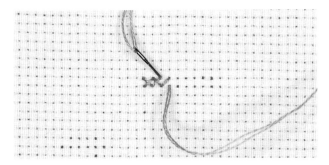

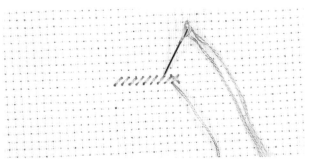

5. Cross over and create an "X" by inserting through the upper left-hand corner hole.

6. You can always stitch multiple stitches at a time, especially if you have a large block of color ahead of you. To do this, repeat steps 1 and 2, creating a line of the first leg and then return to repeat steps 3 and 4. See the figure above. It doesn't really matter if you start in the bottom left, right, or center of your fabric, as long as you make sure that the first leg of your X is always the same.

Another fractional stitch, this stitch looks more like an off-kilter "T." This can help with creating the illusion of curves in a pattern.

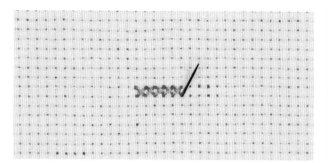

1. Draw your threaded needle up through the back of your fabric.

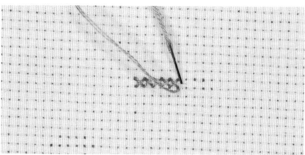

2. Instead of inserting the needle into the diagonal hole, you'll actually push it through the center of the square.

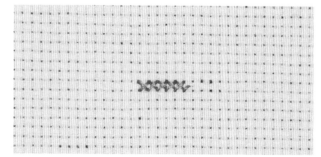

3. This quarter stitch is the first mini leg of your stitch.

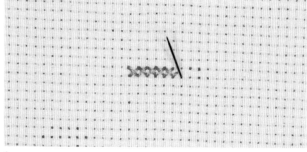

4. Finish the second part of the stitch as you would a traditional cross-stitch leg. Draw your needle up from the backside in the adjacent hole.

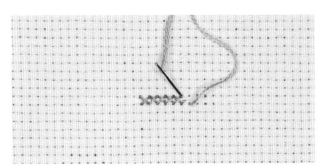

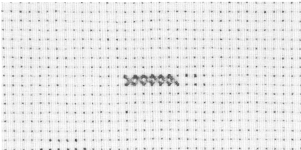

5. Cross over and insert your needle into a diagonal hole.

6. Pull taut to finish.

BACK STITCH

Backstitching is like outlining your pattern. It's really easy and makes your piece look super-professional and finished when it's done. But you can always ditch it if you're not feeling it!

Try to move just one box at a time, but sometimes a pattern will require you to move diagonally or cover multiple stitches. This is fine; do whatever you think looks best for outlining your patterns.

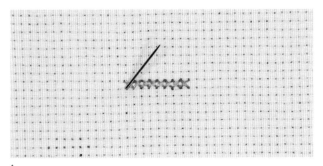

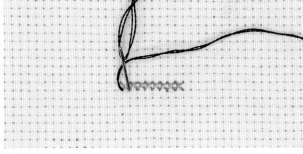

1. Draw your threaded needle up through the bottom left-hand hole of a stitch.

2. Insert through the hole directly to the right of where you came up, the bottom right-hand hole of that box.

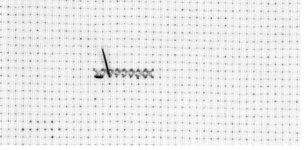

3. Draw your needle through the back side of the fabric in the next square's bottom right-hand hole.

4. Now you'll work left (or "back"), inserting into the hole directly to the left, horizontally.

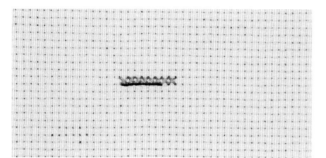

5. Continue working forward then back to make an outline.

FINISHING A PIECE

What to do with your finished work of art? Tons of things. You can frame it, keep it in the hoop, or if you're feeling adventurous, experiment with other creative ideas like adding it to a pillow, clothing, or more!

If you end up taking your project out of the hoop, I recommend ironing it so you don't have any hoop creases. Iron on low heat on the backside of your project. If that's not quite doing the trick, sandwich your piece between two towels. You can iron on the frontside of your pattern (through the towel) and turn up the heat just a little bit until the creases start to flatten out.

SMELLY CAT

The inspiration for this pattern comes from one of the greatest songs and songstresses of all time. A must-have for any cat lover's household, the finished piece also works as the perfect decor near your furry friend's litter box. Simple and classic, this pattern asks: What are they feeding that cat? This is a great pattern if you're new to cross-stitch.

TIPS

✛ Mark the center of your fabric with a pencil.

✛ Stitch all cross-stitches with two strands of floss.

✛ I recommend stitching the top of the black cat closest to the center grid lines before the telltale stink lines.

Fabric: 14-count Aida

Finished size: 5.36 x 5.86 inches, fits a 6-inch diameter hoop

Difficulty level: Easy

Cross-Stitch

◉ 310 Black

▼ 16 Light Chartreuse

DOESN'T SHARE FOOD

We all have our personal credos; some are about truth and dignity and others are about whether or not to share your fries. I know a certain pizza lover who stands by the latter! Go ahead and have another slice, or five, because it's time to start embracing this mantra.

- Mark the center of your fabric with a pencil.

- Stitch all cross-stitches with two strands of floss.

- I recommend starting with "share" before the rest of the words. Finish with the delicious pizza border.

Fabric: 14-count Aida

Finished size: 5.86 x 5.71 inches, fits a 7-inch diameter hoop

Difficulty level: Easy

Cross-Stitch

◎ 310 Black

◢ 721 MD Orange Spice

◇ 703 Chartreuse

Z 741 MD Tangerine

X 444 DK Lemon

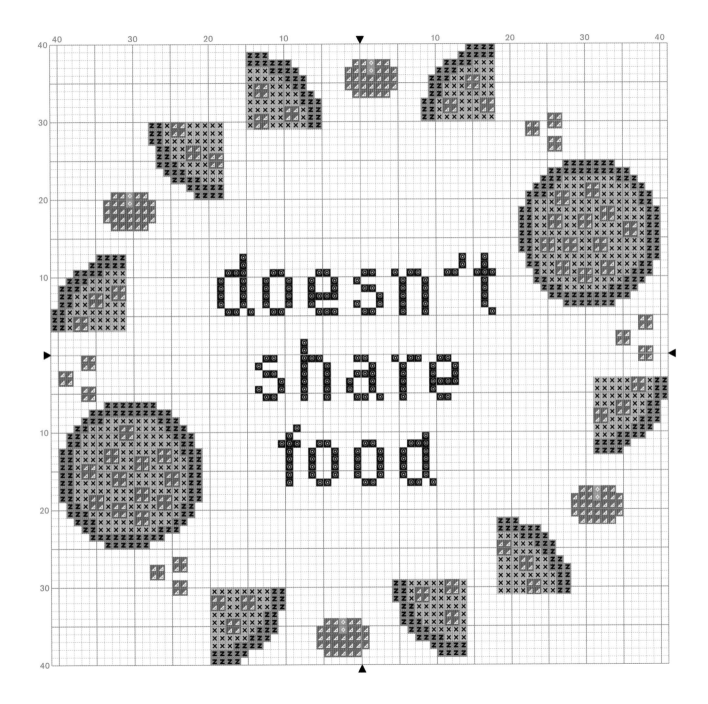

PiVOT

When you find yourself in a tight spot, sometimes you have to adjust your strategy... or pivot! Whether you're trying to move some furniture or just making it through a work day, this pattern will act as a reminder to roll with the punches, and don't be afraid to ask your friends for help. And if all else fails... just cut your couch in half.

TIPS

+ Mark the center of your fabric with a pencil.

+ Stitch all cross-stitches with two strands of floss.

+ I recommend starting with the baby pink "Pivot" before moving on to additional colors.

Fabric: 14-count Aida

Finished size: 6.93 x 3.93 inches, fits a 5 x 7-inch frame

Difficulty level: Easy

Cross-Stitch

⊙ 818 Baby Pink

◆ 892 MD Carnation

Z 304 MD Red

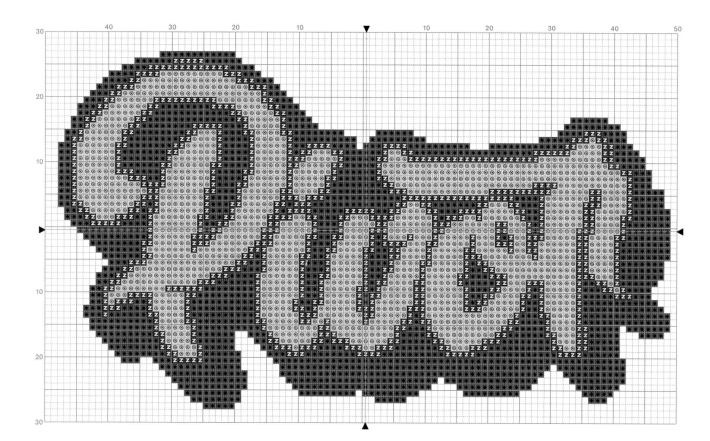

THE CHICK AND THE DUCK

Best friends come in all shapes, sizes, and sometimes species. This adorable pattern makes a great gift for whoever is the chick to your duck.

TIPS

✛ Mark the center of your fabric with a pencil.

✛ Stitch all cross-stitches with two strands of floss.

✛ Since the duck is an off-white color, I recommend using a non-white Aida fabric.

✛ Stitch the duck first before moving to the chick and letters.

Fabric: 14-count Aida

Finished size: 5.79 x 5.14 inches, fits a 7-inch diameter hoop

Difficulty level: Easy

Cross-Stitch

◩ 310 Black

\# 744 Pale Yellow

◆ 762 V LT Pearl Gray

Z 351 Coral

◉ 742 LT Tangerine

◇ 3756 Ultra V LT Baby Blue

HOW YOU DOIN'?

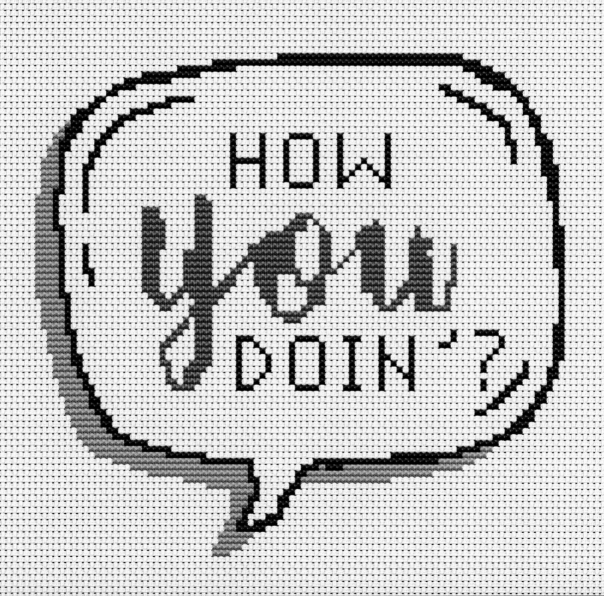

There's a plethora of pickup lines out there to choose from, but this pattern reminds us that sometimes, simple is best. Take a page right out of our favorite New Yorker's playbook and send this hilarious pattern to the next person who catches your eye.

TIPS

+ Mark the center of your fabric with a pencil.

+ Stitch all cross-stitches with two strands of floss.

+ Start with "you" at the center before moving on to the rest of this classic catchphrase. Leave the black and blue border for last.

Fabric: 14-count Aida

Finished size: 6.36 x 5.86 inches, fits a 7-inch diameter hoop or 7 x 7-inch frame

Difficulty level: Easy

Cross-Stitch

◉ 310 Black

◈ 961 DK Dusty Rose

Z 3845 MD Bright Turquoise

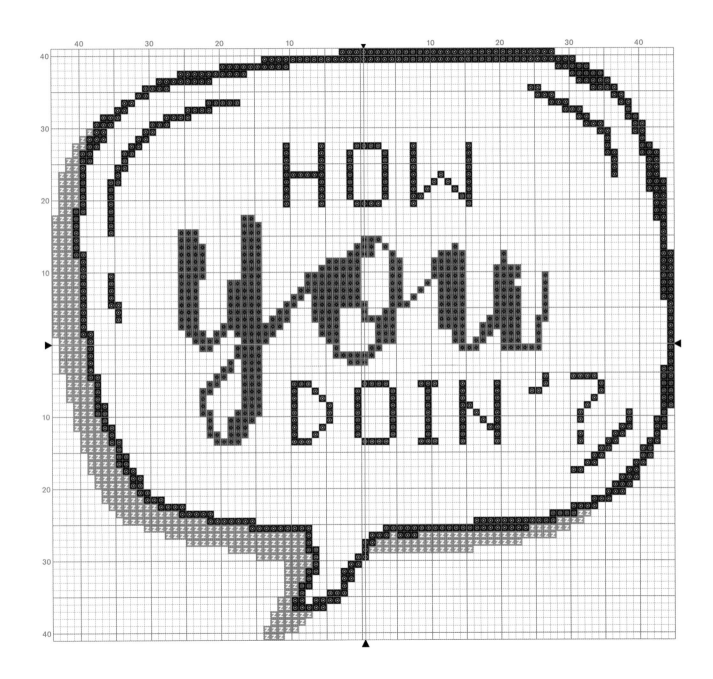

UNAGi

Unagi definitely means freshwater eel and is definitely not a martial arts technique. Enjoying an unagi roll may not put you in a state of total awareness, but it's sure delicious.

TIPS

✦ Mark the center of your fabric with a pencil.

✦ Stitch all cross-stitches with two strands of floss.

✦ The sushi rice color is off-white, but if you really want this pattern to pop you can use a non-white Aida fabric.

✦ Begin with the rice part of the pattern closest to the blue center grid lines before moving on to the face and unagi topping. Save the text for last.

Fabric: 14-count Aida

Finished size: 3.71 x 4.14 inches, fits a 5-inch diameter hoop

Difficulty level: Easy

Cross-Stitch

◎ 535 V LT Ash Gray

◆ 742 LT Tangerine

746 Off White

▼ 920 MD Copper

Z 819 LT Baby Pink

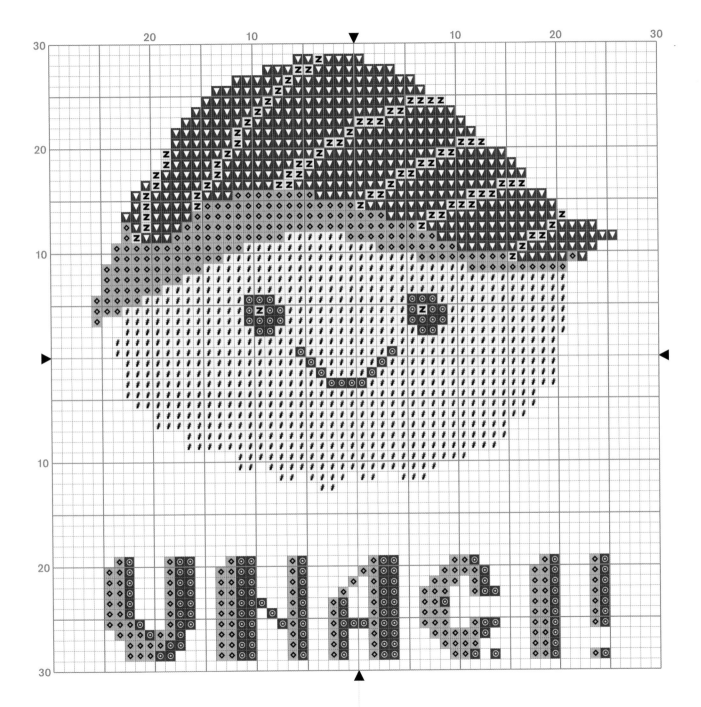

I'LL BE THERE FOR YOU

I'LL BE

THERE

FOR YOU

44

If we've learned anything from ten seasons of hilarious city-life adventures, quirky holiday parties, and emotional breakups and reunions, it's that your friends will always be there for you. So, stitch this pattern for the friend who will stay by your side through thick and thin.

- ✛ Mark the center of your fabric with a pencil.

- ✛ Stitch all cross-stitches with two strands of floss.

- ✛ I recommend starting with the word "there" before moving on to the rest of the lyrics and border.

- ✛ Make sure to give yourself extra fabric along the edges so you can frame this one nicely!

Fabric: 14-count Aida

Finished size: 3.86 x 4.86 inches, fits a 4 x 6-inch frame

Difficulty level: Easy

Cross-Stitch

◉ 310 Black

✖ 3849 LT Teal Green

◢ 745 LT Pale Yellow

◈ 352 LT Coral

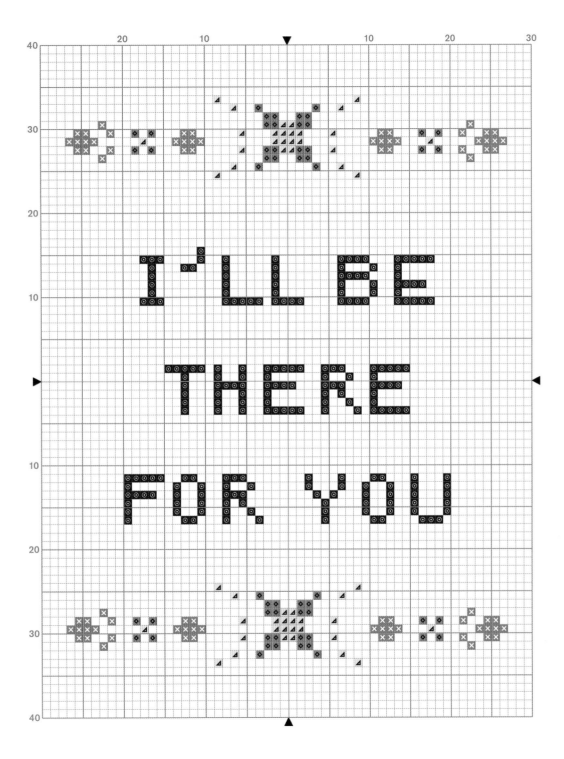

MOO POINT

1.8

When life gets tough, this comical pattern will remind you not to get hung up on the moo points. That person doesn't like you? Who cares? That's a moo point—aka a cow's opinion—and therefore, it doesn't matter.

+ Mark the center of your fabric with a pencil.

+ Stitch all cross-stitches with two strands of floss.

+ The cow's bell is a good starting point, even though it's not quite center. Leave the text for last.

+ Make sure to give yourself extra fabric along the edges so you can frame this one nicely!

Fabric: 14-count Aida

Finished size: 5.36 x 5.43 inches, fits a 7-inch diameter hoop

Difficulty level: Easy

Cross-Stitch

◆ 3750 V DK Antique Blue

▼ 3865 Winter White

♥ 3326 LT Rose

⊙ 973 Bright Canary

Z 602 MD Cranberry

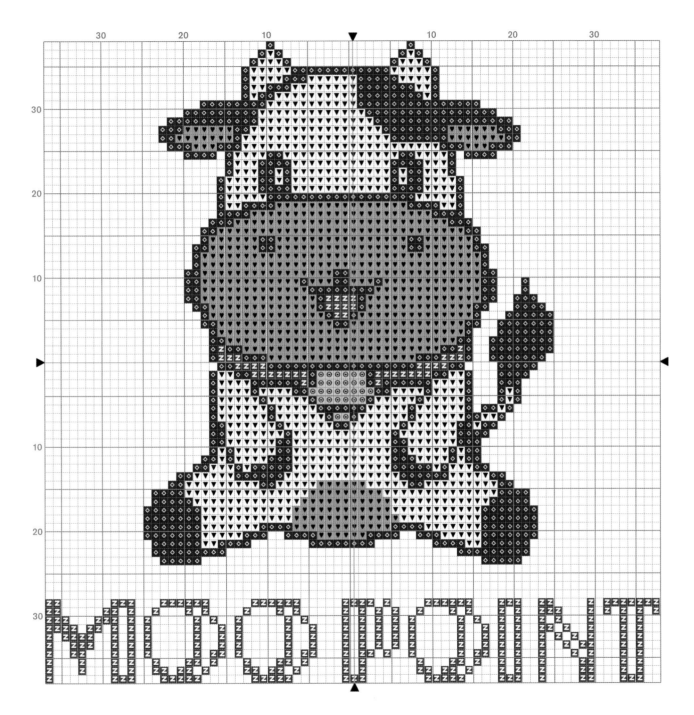

THANKSGIVING TRIFLE

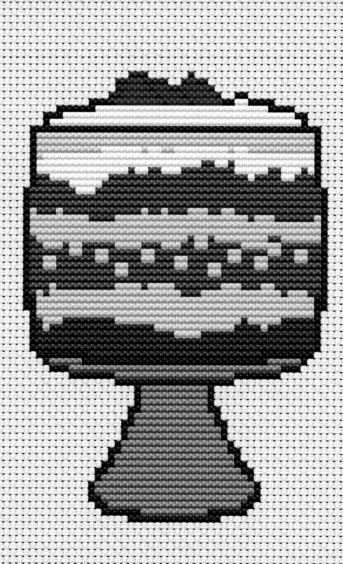

If you're searching for the perfect gift for that special foodie in your life, look no further. Use this pattern to stitch together perhaps the most iconic sitcom holiday food of all time. That special ingredient? Definitely those green peas hiding in one of the layers. Custard? Good. Jam? Good. Meat? GOOD.

+ Mark the center of your fabric with a pencil.

+ Stitch all cross-stitches with two strands of floss.

+ Start with the centermost custard layer before moving on to the other (now-classic) layers!

Fabric: 14-count Aida

Finished size: 3.71 x 6.43 inches, fits a 5 x 7-inch frame

Difficulty level: Easy

Cross-Stitch

▨ 310 Black

✖ 355 DK Terra Cotta

$ 739 Ultra V LT Tan

♥ 3801 V DK Melon

◰ 318 LT Steel Gray

◎ 3860 Cocoa

中 3865 Winter White

⬤ 772 V LT Yellow Green

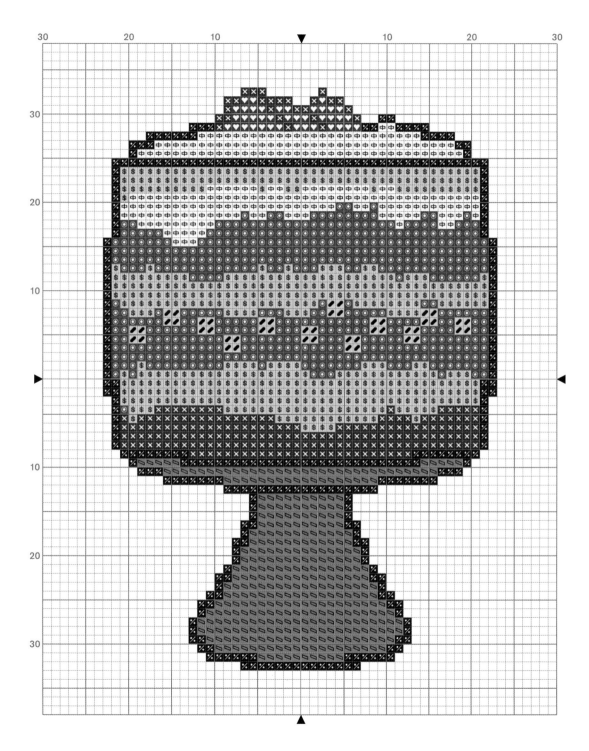

WE WERE ON A BREAK

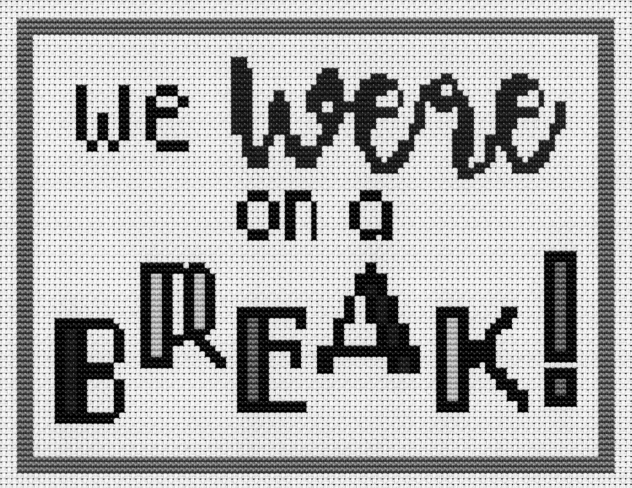

Relationships can be tough. Whether you're somewhere between "single" and "it's complicated," this pattern is your reminder not to forget the all-important "communication."

+ Mark the center of your fabric with a pencil.

+ Stitch all cross-stitches with two strands of floss.

+ Start with "on a" to center the pattern. Work from there out, wherever it's easiest for you to count.

+ If you plan to frame this one, make sure to leave plenty of extra fabric around the edges.

Fabric: 14-count Aida

Finished size: 7.93 x 5.86 inches, fits a 6 x 8-inch frame

Difficulty level: Easy

Cross-Stitch

◯ 310 Black

◈ 666 Bright Red

◉ 3845 MD Bright Turquoise

Z 973 Bright Canary

WE WERE
on a
BREAK!

SEVEN

As a certain obsessive-compulsive chef once said, it's not just about the seven, but the journey you take to get to the seven. This pattern is your reminder to mix and match some ones, twos, and threes, and to not skip over the fours, fives, and sixes before finally settling on the seven, seven, SEVEN. If you know, you know.

TIPS

+ Mark the center of your fabric with a pencil.

+ Stitch all cross-stitches with two strands of floss.

+ Start with the inner 742 LT Tangerine layer of the "Seven" before moving to the outlines.

Fabric: 14-count Aida

Finished size: 7 x 3.29 inches, fits a 6 x 8-inch frame

Difficulty level: Easy

Cross-Stitch

◉ 741 MD Tangerine

◤ 742 LT Tangerine

Z 310 Black

NYC SKYLINE

Ah, New York City. This pattern is perfect for anyone wanting to celebrate the city that's so iconic, it has multiple names—The Big Apple, The City That Never Sleeps, and The City So Nice They Named It Twice. But I know of a certain six friends who know this city as the one with all the memories.

TIPS

- Mark the center of your fabric with a pencil.

- This is one of the patterns that uses a 16-count Aida fabric.

- Stitch all cross-stitches with two strands of floss.

- Start in the center of the skyline, stitching out from there.

- Since there's only one color, make sure to count carefully!

Fabric: 16-count Aida

Finished size: 7 x 4.69 inches, fits a 5 x 7-inch frame

Difficulty level: Medium

Cross-Stitch

Z 310 Black

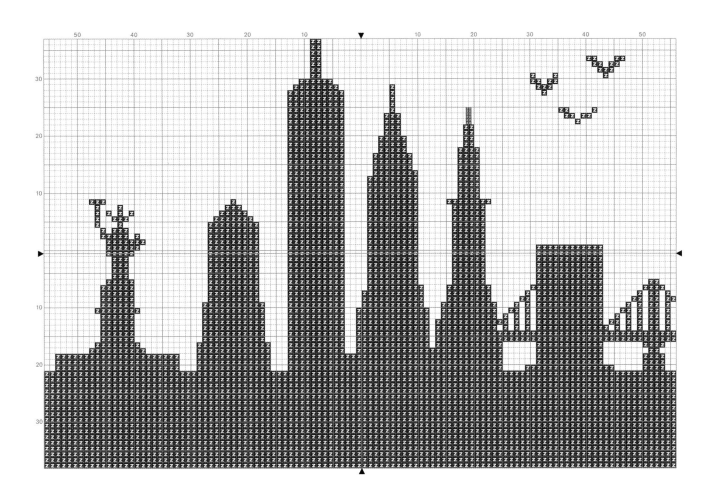

THE YELLOW FRAME

A picture's worth a thousand words, but we all know a picture isn't needed for this charming yellow picture frame that is worth a decade of laughs, smiles, and tears. I mean, could this pattern *be* any more perfect?

+ Mark the center of your fabric with a pencil.

+ Stitch all cross-stitches with two strands of floss.

+ There are no stitches in the center of this pattern, so start from wherever is easiest for you to count.

+ If desired, backstitch with two strands the details and outline of the frame.

Fabric: 14-count Aida

Finished size: 6.21 x 7.07 inches, fits an 8 x 8-inch frame

Difficulty level: Medium

Cross-Stitch

Z 3821 Straw

310 Black

◆ 744 Pale Yellow

⊙ 3865 Winter White

Back Stitch

--- 310 Black 2 strand

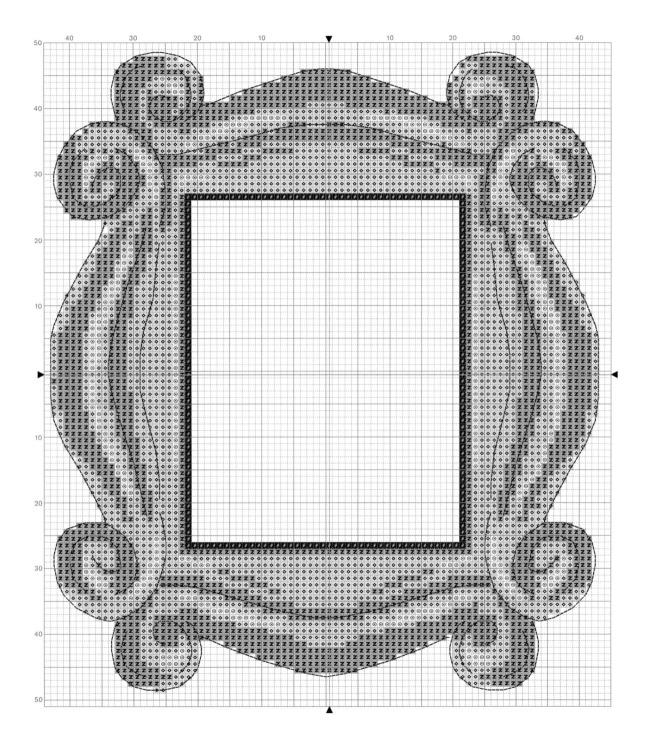

LOBSTER LOVE

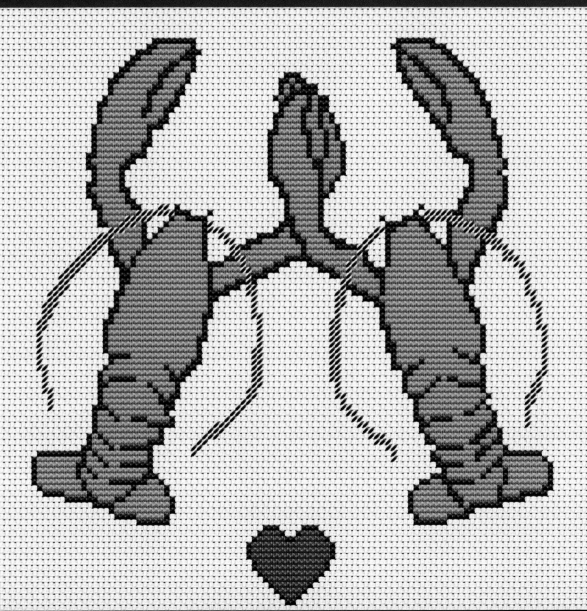

Did you know? Lobsters fall in love and mate for life. And, according to a certain musician/massage therapist, they grow old together, walking around holding claws. Give this cute pattern to the person you consider to be your lobster.

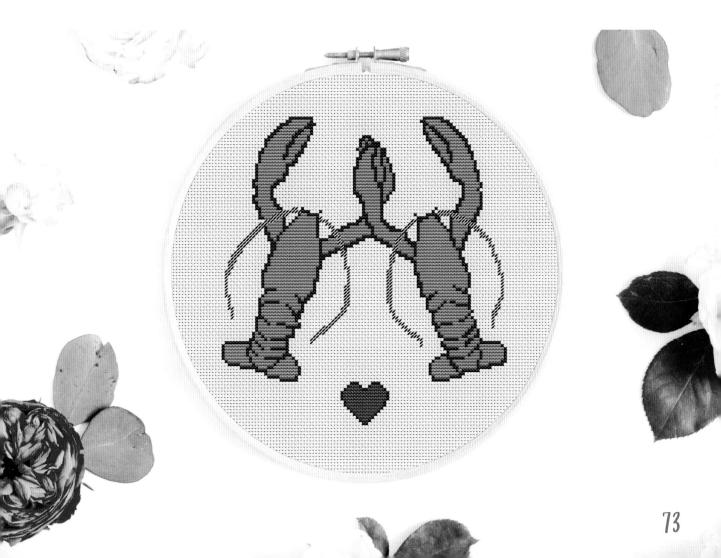

TIPS

+ Mark the center of your fabric with a pencil.

+ Stitch all cross-stitches with two strands of floss.

+ I recommend starting with the 922 LT Copper of one of the lobsters before moving on to other lobster elements and heart. Leave the antennae for last.

+ Half stitch the antennae with two strands.

Fabric: 16-count Aida

Finished size: 5.86 x 6.19 inches, fits a 7-inch diameter loop

Difficulty level: Medium

Cross-Stitch

 # 922 LT Copper

Z 310 Black

◆ 602 MD Cranberry

Half stitch

--- 310 Black 2 strands

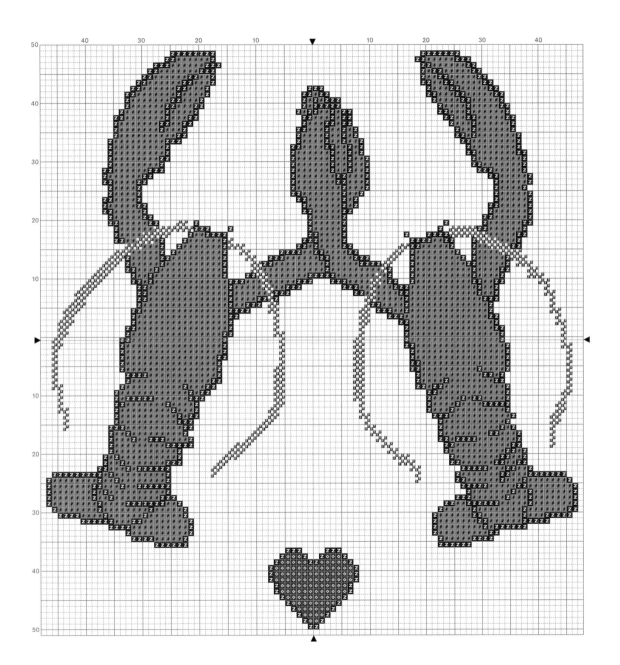

FIRE BEATS EVERYTHING

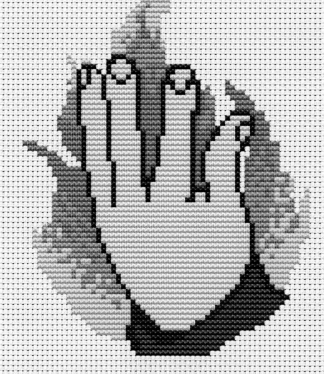

fire beats

EVERYTHING

This is a pattern for rock, paper, scissors champions who know that the key to winning is, of course, FIRE. Fire beats everything... but does it beat water balloon?

TIPS

+ Mark the center of your fabric with a pencil.

+ Stitch all cross-stitches with two strands of floss.

+ Start with the index finger of your favorite native New Yorker. Finish the hand before tackling the flames and text.

Fabric: 14-count Aida

Finished size: 6.71 x 7.29 inches, fits an 8-inch diameter hoop

Difficulty level: Medium

Cross-Stitch

■ 741 MD Tangerine

♥ 742 LT Tangerine

◆ 413 DK Pewter Gray

Z 740 Tangerine

◉ 310 Black

◆ 739 Ultra V LT Tan

GRANDMA'S TAXI

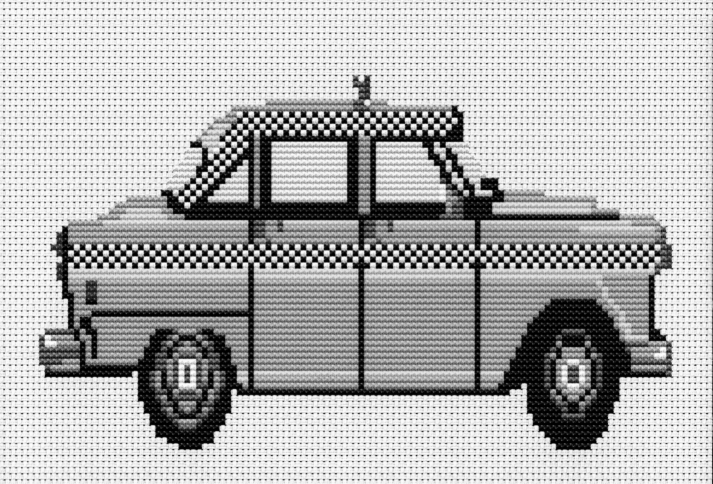

Riding in a New York City taxi is an experience, whether you're hailing a cab to zip through the streets of Manhattan or taking a friend's cab up the mountain for a skiing trip.

TIPS

- ✛ Mark the center of your fabric with a pencil.
- ✛ This pattern uses 16-count Aida fabric.
- ✛ Stitch all cross-stitches with two strands of floss.
- ✛ Start in the center of the pattern using the main yellow color, 972 Deep Canary.
- ✛ Everything here is cross-stitched, but there are a lot of very small details, so make sure to count carefully!

Fabric: 16-count Aida

Finished size: 6.81 x 3.88 inches, fits a 5 x 7-inch frame

Difficulty level: Medium

Cross-Stitch

- ◪ 414 DK Steel Gray
- ◈ 972 Deep Canary
- ♥ 3801 V DK Melon
- # Ecru
- ✖ 310 Black
- ◣ 307 Lemon
- ⊙ 3865 Winter White
- ◆ 415 Pearl Gray

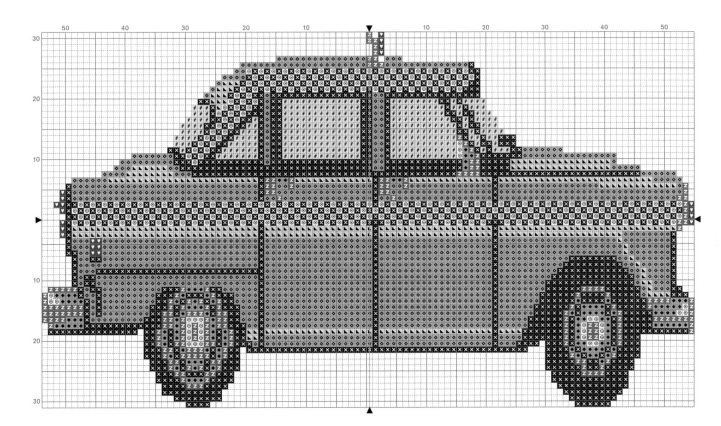

TRANSPONSTERS

Ever have that one friend whose job you just can't remember, no matter how many times they tell you about it? Odds are, they're probably a transponster who works with numbers... or something? Anyway, this pattern is just for them.

TIPS

+ Mark the center of your fabric with a pencil.

+ Stitch all cross-stitches with two strands of floss.

+ I recommend starting with the background banner of "Transponsters" using the 3845 MD Bright Turquoise color.

+ When you've cross-stitched all the elements, there's a small bit of backstitching to top it off. With two strands, backstitch the "INC."

Fabric: 14-count Aida

Finished size: 6.86 x 4.93 inches, fits a 5 x 7-inch or 6 x 8-inch frame

Difficulty level: Medium

Cross-Stitch

◯ 3845 MD Bright Turquoise

◤ 3840 LT Lavender Blue

◣ 666 Bright Red

◉ 3750 V DK Antique Blue

Back Stitch

--- 3750 V DK Antique Blue 2 Strand

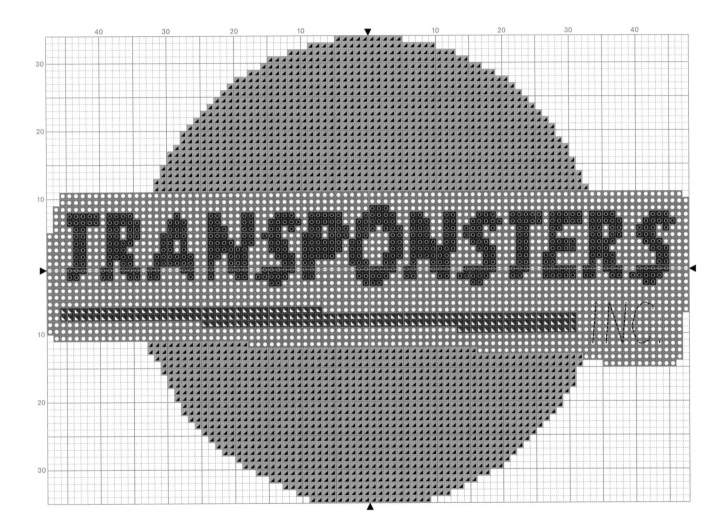

CENTRAL PERK

This iconic little coffee shop taught us what a favorite cafe should be: a go-to spot to gather with friends, your personal stage when performing a commercial jingle or two, and the place you run away to when you get cold feet at the altar.

TIPS

+ Mark the center of your fabric with a pencil.

+ I used an oval hoop since this one is wider than it is tall. Stitch all cross-stitches with two strands of floss.

+ I recommend cross-stitching the green background behind "Perk" first before moving on to the other elements of the pattern.

+ Half stitch with two strands the letters for "Central Perk."

+ If desired, backstitch all elements for a more polished look. Use a 2-strand backstitch to outline the sign.

+ Note: there's a small bit of 1-strand backstitch on the "bolts" next to "Perk" that add a little extra dimension.

Fabric: 14-count Aida

Finished size: 6.79 x 2.36 inches, fits a 5 x 7-inch frame

Difficulty level: Hard

Cross-Stitch

◖ 310 Black

◣ 3852 V DK Straw

◈ 800 Pale Delft Blue

Z 798 DK Delft Blue

1 3818 Ultra V DK Emerald Green

◉ 677 V LT Old Gold

◆ 3743 V LT Antique Violet

Half Stitch

◿ 919 Red Copper

Back Stitch

--- 310 Black 2 Strand

--- 919 Red Copper 2 Strand

···· 798 DK Delft Blue 1 Strand

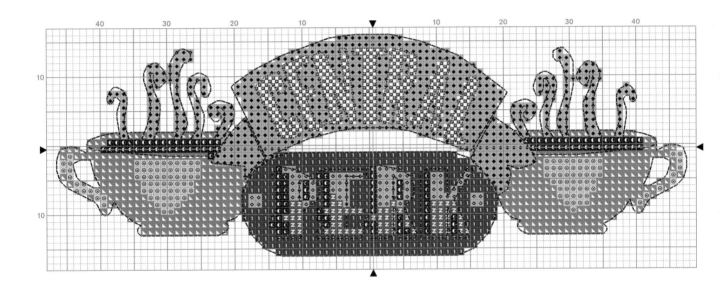

The Turkey

For some, Thanksgiving might mean grandma's famous stuffing, gathering with friends and family, or a much-needed day off from work. But this pattern is for those that think Thanksgiving is the perfect opportunity to shove an uncooked turkey wearing sunglasses and a Fez on your head and do a little dance to impress your crush.

+ Mark the center of your fabric with a pencil.

+ Stitch all cross-stitches with two strands of floss.

+ Start stitching the turkey's body before moving on to the sunglasses and fez.

+ Note the three-quarter and quarter stitches around the edges of the turkey and sunglasses to create a more curved turkey shape. Use two strands when stitching those.

+ Finish with backstitching if desired. Backstitch with 1 strand around the fez's tassel. Use two strands for the outline of the rest of the image.

Fabric: 14-count Aida

Finished size: 4.86 x 6.43 inches, fits a 5 x 7-inch frame

Difficulty level: Hard

Cross-Stitch

◆ 3821 Straw

Z 3770 V LT Tawny

▼ 3863 MD Mocha Beige

◉ 900 DK Burnt Orange

Backstitch

.... 310 Black 1 Strand

--- 310 Black 2 Strand

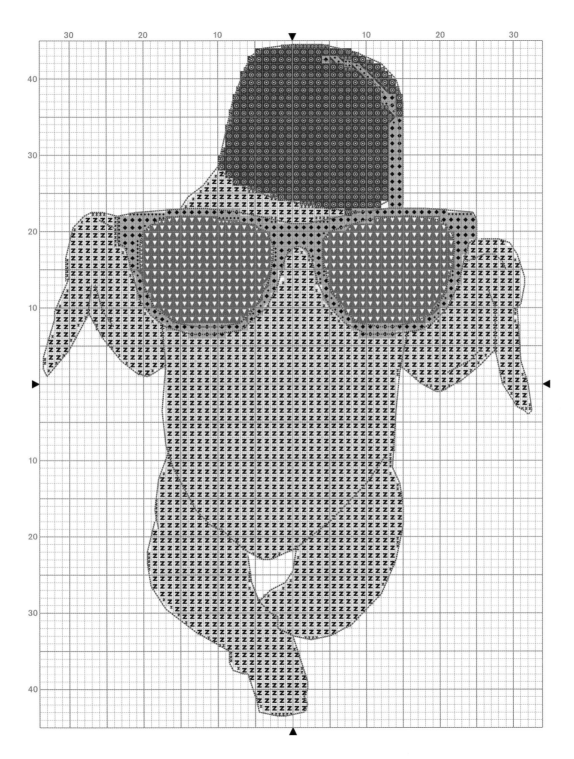

THE COUCH AND LAMP

Inspired by everyone's favorite opening theme song, this pattern will remind you that sometimes you just need to pull your living room furniture out onto your lawn... and maybe jump fully clothed into a fountain.

TIPS

+ Mark the center of your fabric with a pencil.

+ Stitch all cross-stitches with two strands of floss.

+ Begin with the couch before moving on to the lamp.

+ There's a lot of backstitching in this pattern, and I recommend it here for that extra detail. Backstitch with two strands of the 920 MD Copper color to give the arms of the couch extra dimension. Backstitch with one strand of 310 Black to create the iconic tufted cushions. Finish by backstitching with two strands of 310 Black around the couch and lampshade.

Fabric: 14-count

Finished size: 6.07 x 4.21 inches, fits a 5 x 7-inch frame

Difficulty level: Hard

Cross-Stitch

◎ 920 MD Copper

✚ 310 Black

= 414 DK Steel Gray

Z 973 Bright Canary

S 704 Bright Chartreuse

◆ 3853 DK Autumn Gold

♥ 666 Bright Red

◆ 3746 DK Blue Violet

Back Stitch

--- 920 MD Copper 2 Strand

···· 310 Black 2 Strand

--- 310 Black 1 Strand

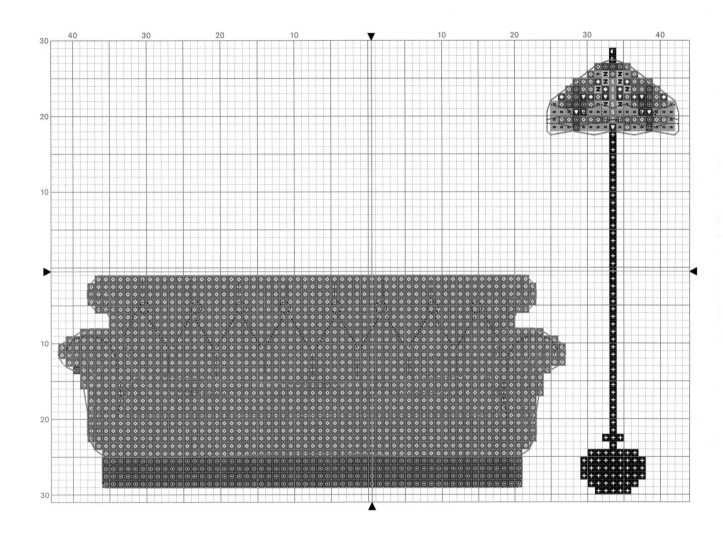

ICONIC ALPHABET

A B C D E F
G H I J K L
M N O P Q R
S T U V W X
Y Z . ! ? 0 1 2
3 4 5 6 7 8 9

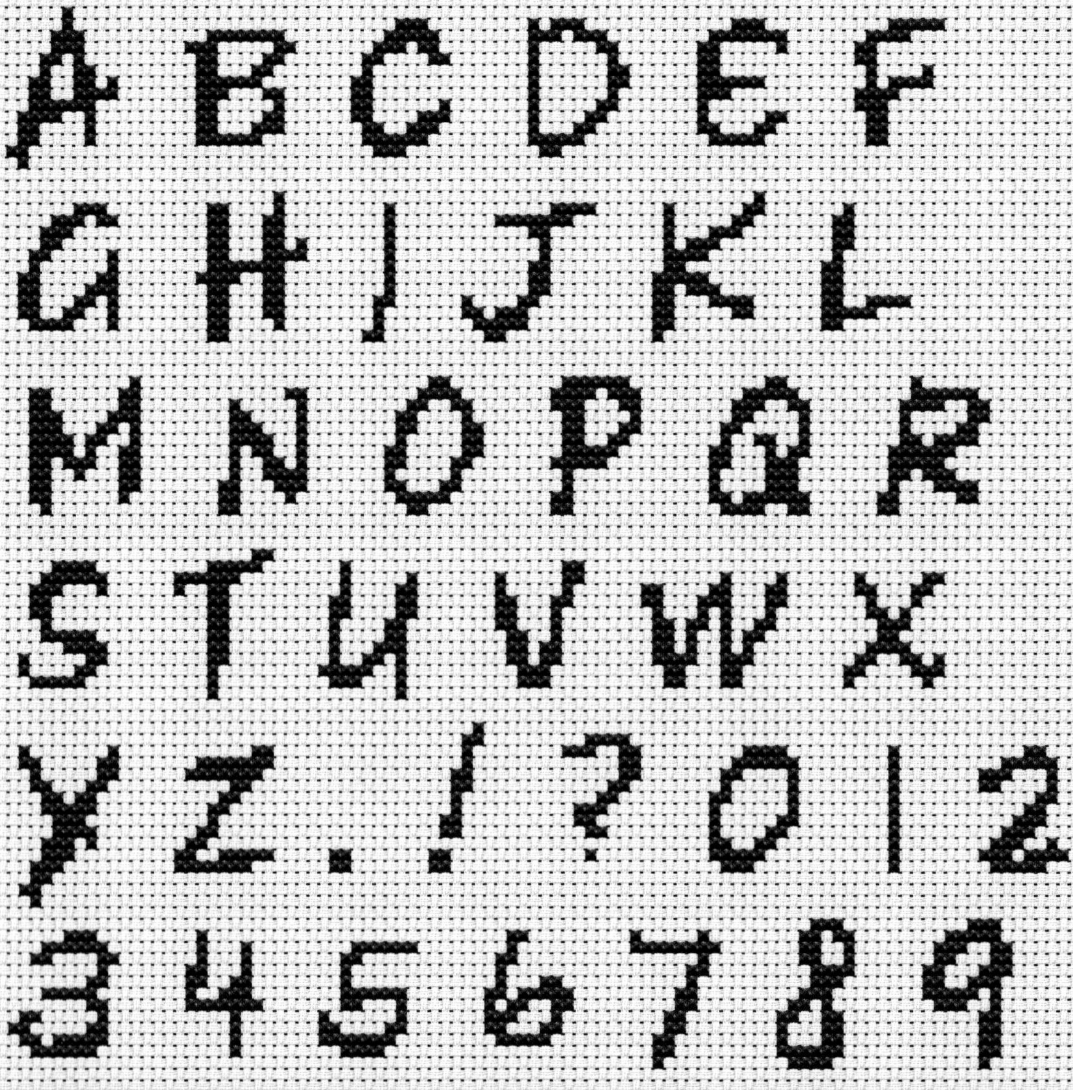

Your favorite catchphrase missing from these patterns? You can do it yourself! Whether it's an Oh. My. God. or something else, create your own timeless patterns with this iconic alphabet.

TIPS

+ You can make this cross-stitch as simple or ornate as you like, so the size and difficulty level is up to you!

Fabric: 14-count Aida

Finished size: n/a

Difficulty level: n/a

Cross-Stitch

⊙ 310 Black

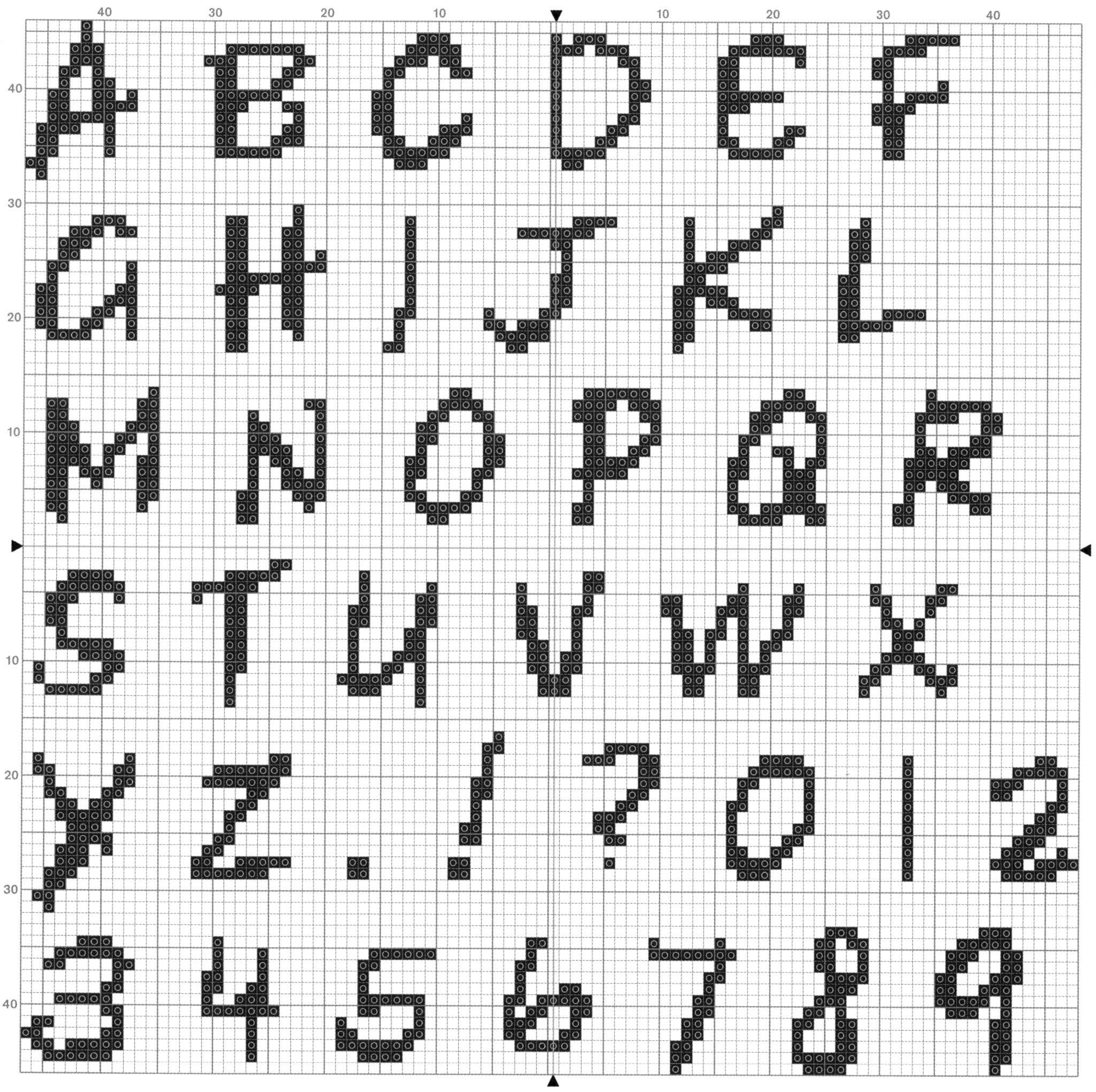
40 30 20 10 10 20 30 40
40 30 20 10 10 20 30 40

ABOUT THE PATTERN DESIGNER

Anna Selezneva aka "AnnyFunnyXx" is a cross-stitch designer and game designer from Russia. All her life she has dreamt of being an artist and, when it came to cross-stitch, it was love at first sight! She has over two thousand patterns in her portfolio and won't stop any time soon. She likes PS games and watching TV. You can find her on Instagram, Facebook, and Etsy as AnnyFunnyXx.